Expressive Etudes

TRADITIONAL STUDIES
FOR ARTISTIC DEVELOPMENT
AT THE PIANO

Book Three

Early Intermediate

Compiled and edited by
Suzanne W. Guy

Practice Suggestions

Posture is critical to good technique. Sit tall and centered on the front part of the bench.

- **Prepare yourself physically using this checklist:**

shoulders	Roll your shoulders forward and back several times. Now lift them toward your ears and let them fall comfortably into place.
upper arms	Dangle your arms at your sides while seated at the piano. Lift them slowly in front of you, parallel to the floor, then drop them freely in your lap.
forearms	Move your forearms rapidly from side to side (similar to erasing), then up and down (as if hammering a nail). You are using horizontal and vertical motion.
wrists	Hold your R.H. fingertips snugly in the palm of your L.H. and move the wrist down and up (repeat several times and then reverse hands). Use this gesture to begin and end phrases.
fingers	Imagine pressing a thumb tack into a cork board with a firm fingertip. First joints should be strong and not collapse.

- **Scan the etude to find the specific technical elements used by the composer.** Practice them slowly and accurately.

- **Notice and observe all markings on the page:** character and tempo indications, dynamics, articulation, and phrase lengths. Attention to these details will bring the etude to life and make it more expressive.

- **Determine a reasonable practice tempo from the most difficult measures.** Then play through the entire etude until it flows.

- **Practice your etude at three different tempi:** slow–medium–fast. A good rule to follow is "two times slow for one time fast."

- **Work at your own tempo and pace,** always playing music, not just the notes. Remember to stress the beauty of the sound, which is more important than speed. Your technical fluency will increase as you continue to practice.

- **Use your imagination.** A scale might represent a beautiful melody sung by your favorite singer. A chord could portray the approach of a powerful dragon. An arpeggio might be a fountain. Come up with your own ideas.

Enjoy the challenges and rewards of etude practice.

Expressive Etudes
Book Three – *Early Intermediate*

Table of Contents

FF1307

The Trumpeter

(A First Book)

Broken triads and inversions; alternating rhythm patterns

Cornelius Gurlitt
(1820–1901)

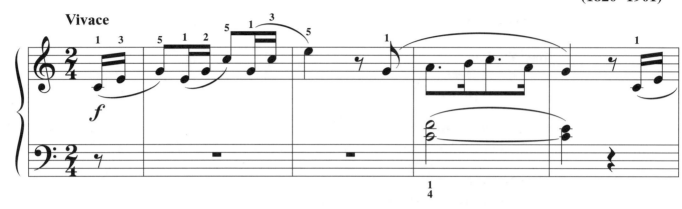

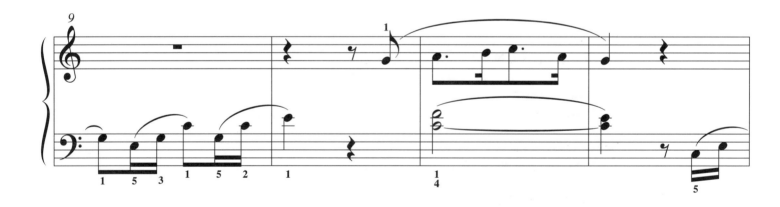

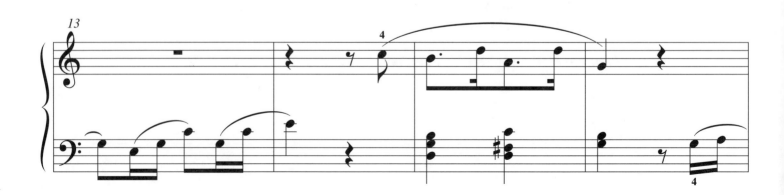

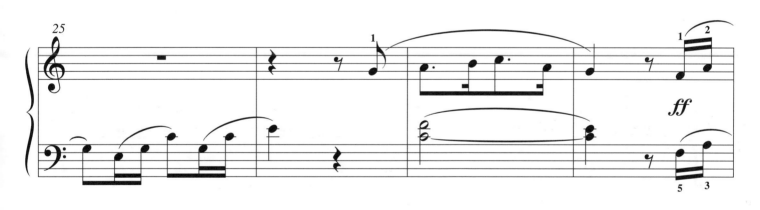

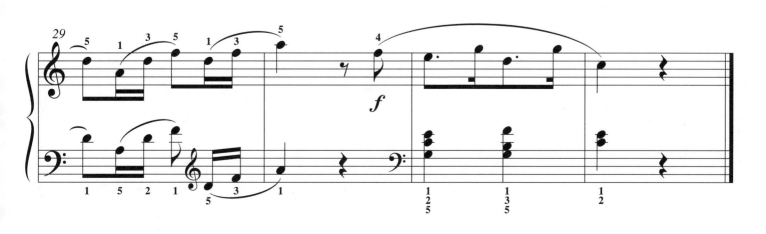

Etude, Op. 82, No. 52

(The First Steps of the Young Pianist)

Color contrast between minor and major scales
approached by octave extension

Cornelius Gurlitt
(1820–1901)

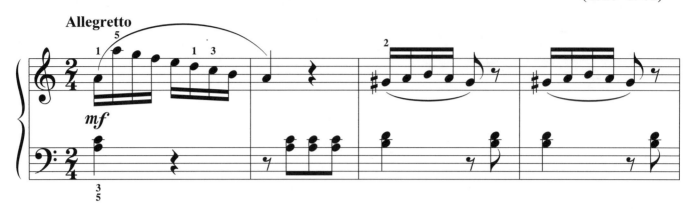

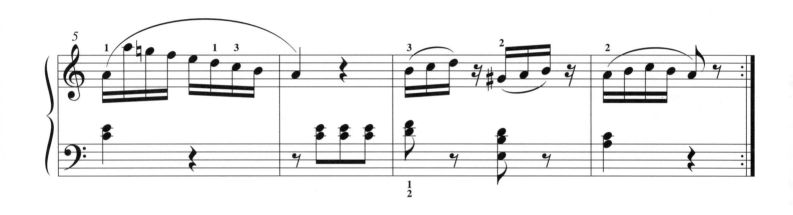

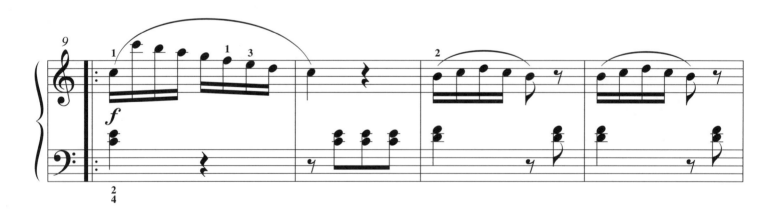

Écossaise

Cantabile melodic lines; legato broken octaves;
balance of chordal accompaniment

Franz Schubert
(1797–1828)

Etude, Op. 777, No. 18

(Five-finger Studies)

Voicing of thirds; waltz pattern with sustained bass

Carl Czerny
(1791–1857)

Etude, Op. 823, No. 19
(The Little Pianist)

L.H. triplets; circular wrist motion

Carl Czerny
(1791–1857)

(light pedal optional)

Etude, Op. 599, No. 50

(Practical Method for Beginners)

R.H. thirds; L.H. scale patterns

Carl Czerny
(1791–1857)

Etude, Op. 89, No. 4

(25 Studies for the Left Hand)

L.H. alone; expansion and contraction; forearm motion

Hermann Berens
(1826–1880)

Staccato

Two-note slurs; quick release of wrist and finger staccato

Carl Reinecke
(1824–1910)

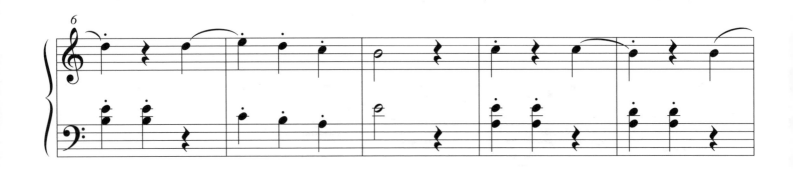

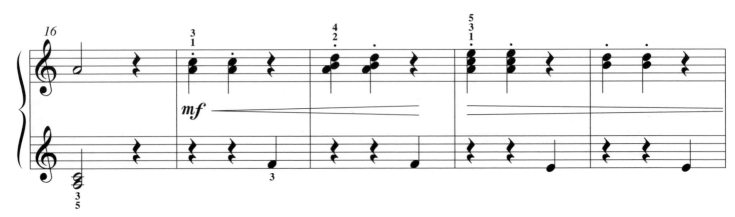

Etude, Op. 17, No. 12

(The Alphabet—25 Very Easy Studies)

Single–line cantabile melody; repeated–note chordal accompaniment

Felix Le Couppey
(1811–1887)

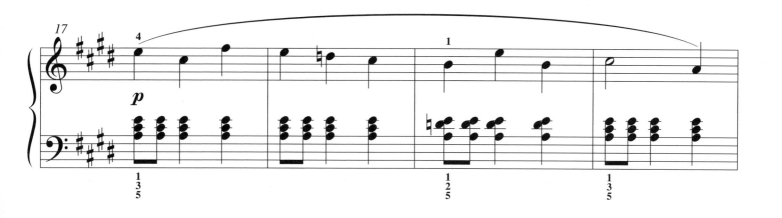

D.C. al Fine

Distant Bells, Op. 63, No. 6

(12 Melodious Pieces, Book 1)

Bell tones on L.H. crossing; R.H. double–note rotation

Jean Louis Streabbog
(1835–1886)

By the Seaside, Op. 63, No. 7

(12 Melodious Pieces, Book 1)

Broken chords; harmonic pedaling in A section

Jean Louis Streabbog
(1835–1886)

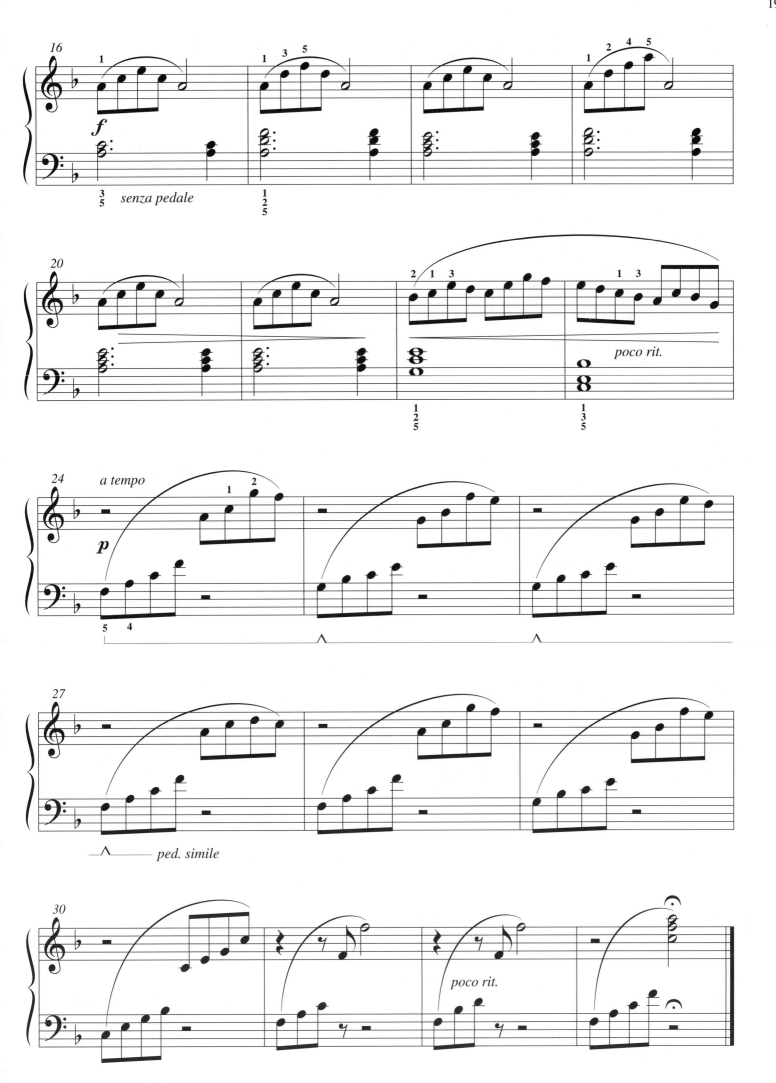

The Orphan, Op. 64, No. 4

(12 Melodious Pieces, Book 2)

Cantabile melody; grace notes; flowing accompaniment

Jean Louis Streabbog
(1835–1886)

22

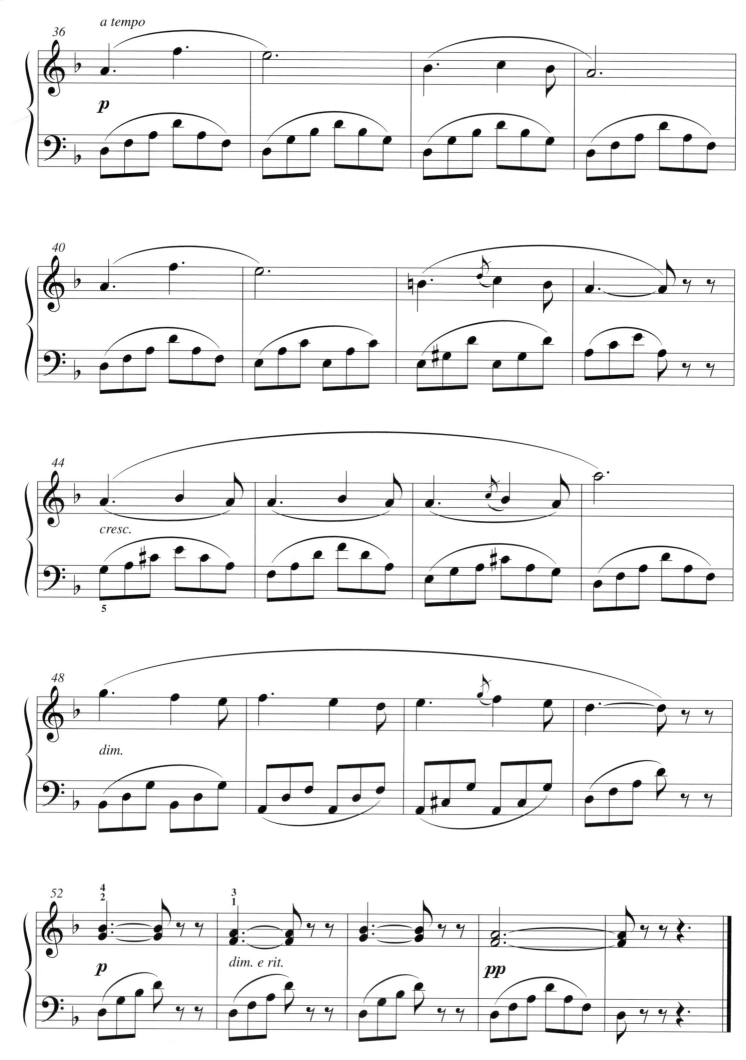

Melody, Op. 68, No. 1

(Album for the Young)

Flowing legato; R.H. melody throughout
doubled by a L.H. hidden melody

Robert Schumann
(1810–1856)

The fingerings shown in italics are Schumann's own.

Study, Op. 176, No. 24

(25 Elementary Studies)

Bouncing sixths and thirds; staccato repeated notes

Jean-Baptiste Duvernoy
(1802–1880)

Study, Op. 13, No. 8

(12 Little Fantasy Studies)

Melodic transfer; repeated intervals; dotted rhythms; key and tempo change

Alec Rowley
(1892–1958)

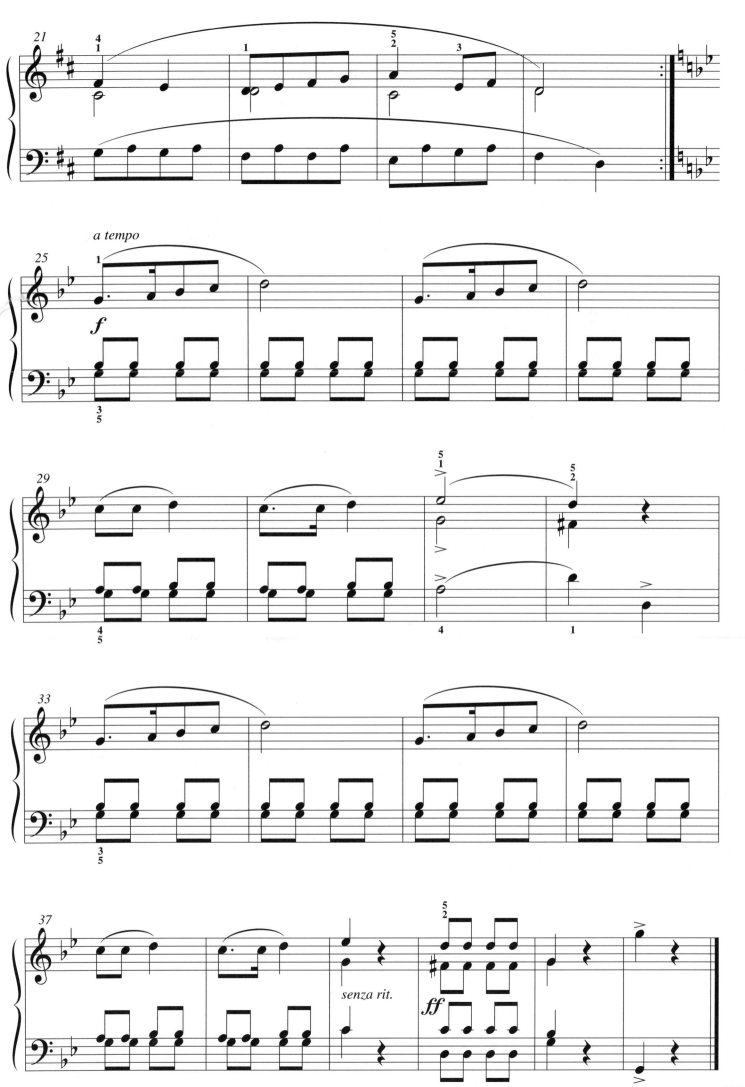

Study, Op. 176, No. 21

(25 Elementary Studies)

Continuous E♭ major scales; accents

Jean-Baptiste Duvernoy
(1802–1880)

Allegro Deciso

(For Children, Vol. 1)

Syncopation; tenuto and staccato contrast;
wrist and finger staccato

Béla Bartók
(1881–1945)

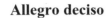

Allegro deciso

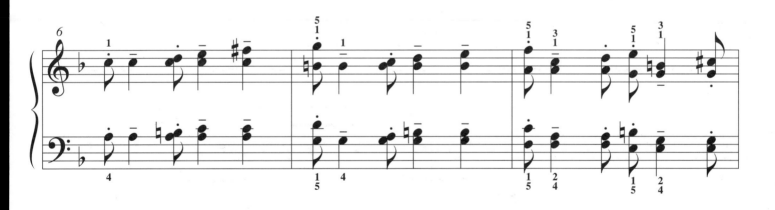

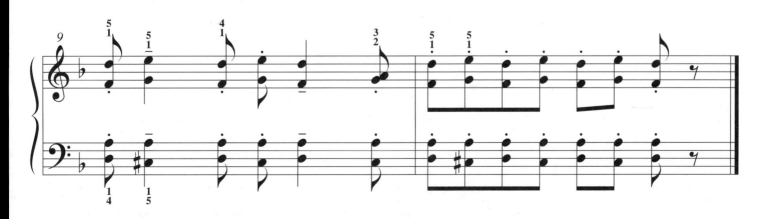

Round Dance

L.H. written–out trills; broken thirds rotation

Béla Bartók
(1881–1945)

Composer Biographies

Béla Bartók (1881–1945, Hungary) One of the most original composers of the early 20th century, Bartók was also a pianist, teacher, linguist, ethnomusicologist, and editor. He wrote music from the elementary to the virtuosic level, including three piano concerti. His pedagogical masterpiece *Mikrokosmos* is a laboratory of 153 miniature pieces incorporating his technical ideas and ethnic spirit.

Hermann Berens (1826–1880, Germany) A pianist and pedagogue who studied with Carl Czerny, Berens composed many etude collections, the most famous of which is the *Training of the Left Hand,* Op. 89. He settled in Sweden and taught composition at the Stockholm Conservatory.

Carl Czerny (1791–1857, Austria) This piano teacher, pianist, and writer composed over a thousand compositions and holds the distinction of writing more exercises and etudes than any other composer. As a pupil of Beethoven and the primary teacher of Liszt, Czerny occupies a unique historical place in the development of piano technique. His technical pieces ensure his legacy.

Jean-Baptiste Duvernoy (1802–1880, France) Although a lesser-known French composer, pianist, and teacher, Duvernoy was interested in the development of piano technique from the earliest levels up to and including intermediate–level piano studies in Op. 120. The 25 etudes in Op. 176 are especially appealing to young pianists.

Cornelius Gurlitt (1820–1901, Austria) An outstanding organist and composer, Gurlitt composed chamber music that included song cycles, a cello sonata, and three violin sonatas. The lyricism in Gurlitt's technical compositions, suggestive of Robert Schumann, appeals to students of all ages.

Felix Le Couppey (1811–1887, France) A man of many talents, Le Couppey was a pianist, teacher, composer, and publisher. He wrote several piano methods while teaching piano and harmony at the Paris Conservatory. His etudes, character pieces, and songs are lyrical as well as technical.

Carl Reinecke (1824–1910, Germany) A professor of music at the famed Leipzig Conservatory, Reinecke wrote music of a pedagogical nature, using technical titles such as "staccato."

Alec Rowley (1892–1958, England) Composer, pianist, and English teacher, Rowley was committed to the musical education of young people. He was half of a concertizing duet team and wrote several concerti for solo instruments and orchestra. His fantasy studies have a distinctive style and sound.

Franz Schubert (1797–1828, Austria) In a lifespan of only 31 years, Schubert was one of the most prolific composers who ever lived. In addition to hundreds of dances, impromptus, sonatas, and miscellaneous works for the piano, he composed more than 600 art songs that are frequently heard in concert. He was adored by friends and patrons who gathered in members' homes for evening musicales (Schubertiaden) to hear Franz play original solos and chamber music, accompany singers, and improvise dance music.

Robert Schumann (1810–1856, Germany) In addition to composing symphonies, a concerto, chamber music, and a large body of piano tone poems, Schumann founded a literary journal that railed against the "lightweight" salon music of his day. Even his simplest compositions (from *Album for the Young*) bear the mark of a complex composer—counterpoint, dotted rhythms, and unusual harmonies.

Jean Louis Streabbog (1835–1886, Belgium) This prolific composer and pianist who taught at the Brussels Conservatory wrote more than a thousand light piano pieces. Streabbog is the pen name for Gobbaerts (spelling it in reverse). Nearly all piano students cut their technical teeth on the melodious studies in Op. 63. Because they were so popular, he wrote a second set in Op. 64 (which was less successful).